In Search of
TROY

In Search of
TROY

One man's quest for Homer's fabled city

Written and illustrated by
Giovanni Caselli

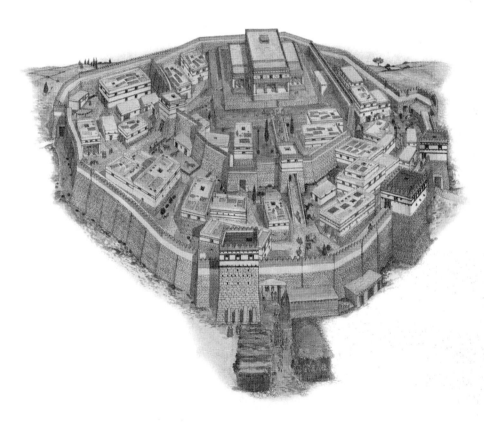

W
FRANKLIN WATTS
NEW YORK•LONDON•SYDNEY

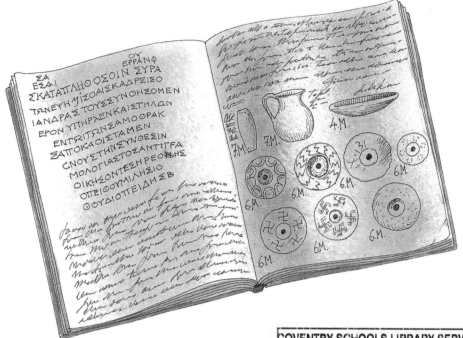

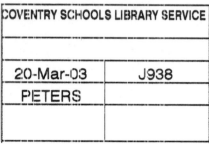

For Kenneth and James

First published in 1999
by Franklin Watts
96 Leonard Street
London
EC2A 4RH

Franklin Watts Australia
14 Mars Road
Lane Cove
NSW 2066

ISBN 0 7496 3110 4

Dewey classification: 939

Printed in Hong Kong / China

Acknowledgments:
The author and publishers would like to thank
Professor Anthony Bonanno of Malta University for
checking the text; and A.C.T.A. Florence for use of the
photographs on pages 36-37.

Contents

A boy's dream

The ancient city of Troy, situated in present-day Turkey, was first settled around 3000BC. It was occupied, built and rebuilt by generation after generation. In about 1240BC it was attacked by the ancestors of the ancient Greeks, the Achaeans. They sailed with 1,000 ships and besieged the city during the historic Trojan War.

Homer, the first and one of the greatest of all poets, lived in Greece around 700BC. He wrote the *Iliad* - a famous poem that describes this great ten-year battle.

In 1829, more than 2,000 years later, a boy called Heinrich Schliemann read the *Iliad*, and dreamed that he would one day discover the remains of the ancient city of Troy.

Aeneas's escape

The Trojan War was celebrated throughout the ancient world. In the *Aeneid*, the Roman poet Virgil told the story of Aeneas, a Trojan hero who escaped from blazing Troy with his young son Ascanius while carrying his ailing father Anchises on his shoulders. Aeneas settled in Italy and his descendants are said to have founded Rome.

Homer and the *Iliad*

Homer, the greatest of Greek poets, was blind. According to legend, he sang his poems at the courts of kings and nobles. In actual fact, scholars believe the *Iliad* was written by no less than two poets who lived around 700BC in one of the Greek cities on the coast of present-day Turkey.

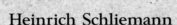

Marble bust of Homer

Heinrich Schliemann

Heinrich Schliemann was born in 1822, the son of a poor German clergyman. When he was seven years old he was given an illustrated "Universal History". One day, looking at a picture of Troy in flames, he said to his father: "Father, if such walls once existed, they cannot have been completely destroyed: vast ruins must still remain hidden away beneath the dust of ages." From these early beginnings, Schliemann's interest in Troy grew into a lifelong obsession.

The search begins

Schliemann left school at the age of 14, and spent the next 30 years travelling the world, educating himself and making money in different ways.

As a young man living in Amsterdam, Schliemann taught himself several languages, including Latin and Greek. Later, he studied the works of Homer and became an "antiquarian" - the 19th-century word for an archaeologist. His early interest in Troy now became a quest to find the lost city.

At this time, the noblemen of Europe had developed a great enthusiasm for the Greek world, and ancient works were being translated for the first time.

Warlike beginnings

In 1798 the French general Napoleon invaded Egypt. Scholars who followed him there made the ruins of ancient Egypt known to the world, helping to popularize archaeology.

Hard study

Schliemann spent long hours trying to work out the location of Troy.

Schliemann as a wealthy young man

Buried mystery

Troy's exact location was unknown. However, 19th-century experts agreed that if the ancient city ever really existed, its ruins must lie buried somewhere in the region of Turkey historically known as "Troas".

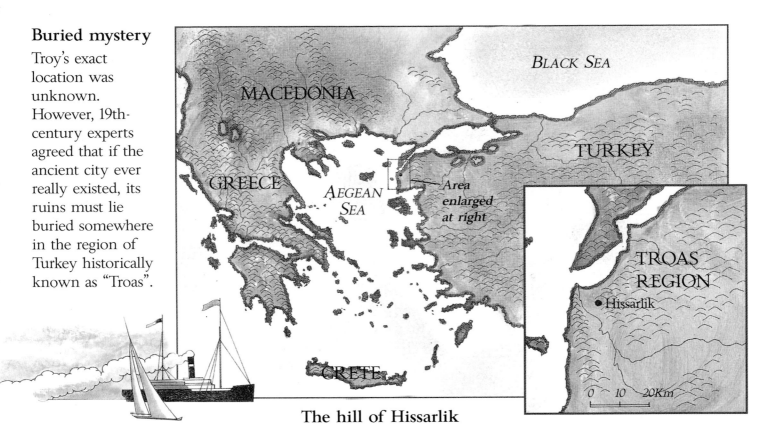

The best way to travel to Greece or Turkey in the 1860s was by steamer

The hill of Hissarlik

Hissarlik had been first studied in 1820s by the antiquarian Charles McLaren. McLaren became convinced that the hill hid the ruins of Troy, but no excavation was started.

In 1869 Schliemann travelled to Greece and married a young woman named Sophia Kastromenos. Together, they set off for Turkey.

In the Troas region, Schliemann began work with a compass in one hand and a copy of the *Iliad* in the other. A hill north of the town of Bunarbashi finally attracted his attention. Its name was Hissarlik, which in Turkish means "the palace".

13

The first digs

Frank Calvert

Hard at work

Schliemann became the first person to test an ancient myth by excavating an archaeological site.

The top of the hill at Hissarlik was an oval plateau 240 metres (770 feet) across. Schliemann got permission to dig there in 1871.

Before work could begin, however, Schliemann had to overcome a problem. The American antiquarian, Frank Calvert, owned part of the hill. He had been the first to realize that Hissarlik was in fact an artificial mound, composed of layers of ruins. Calvert had started his own excavations, convinced that Troy lay beneath. Later, Calvert and Schliemann made an agreement allowing the German to dig on Calvert's part of the hill on condition that all finds would be shared equally.

The Schliemanns built sheds to serve as home, workshop and storehouse

Workers sifted soil in the search for buried artefacts

Digging the hill

A large team of Greek and Turkish hired labourers dug into the mound, using crude spades and picks. They carelessly ripped down walls that looked unimportant.

Detailed drawings

Two pages from Schliemann's notebook show how he accurately drew every object found. This is a vital part of modern archaeology.

Sun god sculpture

In 1872 Schliemann found this relief (flat sculpture) of Helios, the sun god, in a temple on the site. He and Calvert argued over who owned it until Schliemann eventually paid Calvert 200 dollars.

Surveyors helped to map the site

Visitors

Schliemann and his wife worked on the site relentlessly. Many people, such as government officials, antiquarians and journalists, visited them frequently.

Troy and treasure

By 1873 Schliemann realized that many cities had been built on the same site, one on top of the other. The great excavation trench had cut through several of them and was now well below the level of King Priam's Troy.

Exciting finds were being made all the time, but there was still no sign of "Priam's treasure". In the *Iliad* Homer describes the magnificent jewellery worn by Queen Helen at Priam's court. Schliemann had convinced himself that he would find the treasure during the excavation. Only by discovering Priam's treasure could he be sure that he had found Troy and fulfilled his boyhood dreams.

Schliemann at work

A huge trench cut through the hill

Destroying evidence
These huge jars found by Schliemann's workers were soon smashed by local peasants searching for treasures.

Then one hot May morning the labourers, working nine metres (28 feet) below ground level, scraped the foundations of what Schliemann believed to be King Priam's palace. Further digging revealed the lid of a stone chest.

Schliemann and his wife sent the workers away, then plunged into the trench and started digging around the chest with knives. They lifted the lid to reveal the silver and gold of King Priam's long-lost treasure.

Fabulous treasure

Priam's treasure became one of the most famous in history. Buried under the walls of the king's lost city, it had lain undisturbed for more than 3,000 years.

Puzzle hill

Wilhelm Dorpfeld was a young German architect who joined Schliemann at Troy in later seasons. He confirmed that there had been not two or three Troys, but nine cities. These had been built, one upon the ruins of the other, on the hill of Hissarlik between 3000BC and AD500.

Wilhelm Dorpfeld

Found at last

Heinrich and Sophia Schliemann found the treasure in a coffin-shaped chest made of stone.

Priam's Troy

The site of Troy was well chosen. Each time the city was destroyed, by a war or a natural disaster such as an earthquake, it was rebuilt and enlarged.

Most archaeologists now believe that the Troy that Priam knew lasted from 1800-1240BC. Priam himself must have lived towards the end of this period.

The inner city of Priam's Troy, with its stunning buildings, was one of the finest cities in the ancient world. It reached its most splendid period from 1425-1300BC. Homer described Troy as "well built, finely towered and lofty gated".

Parapet made of sun-dried brick protected defenders

Wall construction

Schliemann described the walls as "splendid". They were constructed of closely fitted limestone blocks, with a parapet on the top. This method of construction was typical of the region.

Large limestone blocks

Magnificent tower

The "great tower of Ilios", as Homer named it, was built next to the main gate, called the "Scaean gate". The tower had a wavy top, built of sun-dried mud brick, while the lower part was made of finely hewn limestone blocks. The ground floor room of the tower was probably a shrine - it contained an important altar beside a deep well.

Outer wall

A dry ditch surrounded the outer wall

CUTAWAY OF TOWER AND WALLS

Core of wall made from rubble (loose stones)

Altar and well

Scaean gateway

Wall faced with limestone

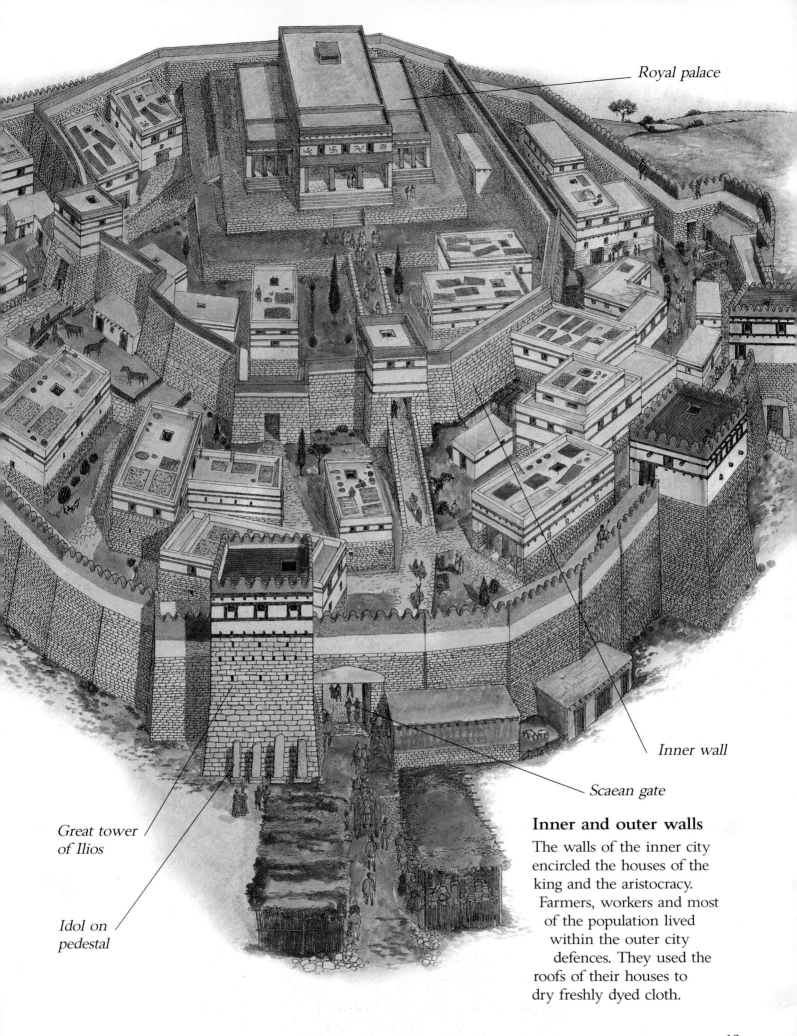

Royal palace

Inner wall

Scaean gate

Great tower
of Ilios

Idol on
pedestal

Inner and outer walls

The walls of the inner city
encircled the houses of the
king and the aristocracy.
Farmers, workers and most
of the population lived
within the outer city
defences. They used the
roofs of their houses to
dry freshly dyed cloth.

Priam's palace

To reach what he claimed was Priam's Troy, Schliemann had cut through later remains, making it difficult to get a clear picture of Priam's city and its buildings. To complicate things further, a later temple had been built on top of what remained of Priam's royal palace.

The inner city had been destroyed by the builders of later structures. But experts can estimate the size of the royal palace from later foundation walls. To make an educated guess at its shape and features, archaeologists studied earlier Trojan remains and the ruins of other royal palaces around the Aegean Sea. Many items that Schliemann recovered also help to give us an idea of what the structure was like.

OBJECTS FOUND BY SCHLIEMANN IN THE PALACE AREA

Two ceramic drinking cups, one decorated with spirals

A decorated ceramic cup stand

This ivory plate was part of a seven-stringed lyre

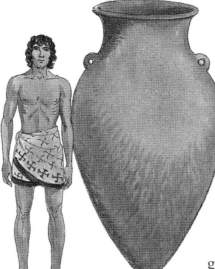

Palace plan

Plan of King Nestor's palace at Pylos. Experts believe this building and Priam's palace may have shared similar features.

Supporting pillars

Four huge wooden pillars on stone bases supported the palace's first-storey beams.

Storage jars

Workers discovered these giant storage jars in almost every house of Priam's Troy. The vessels may have held oil or wine. They were half-buried in the ground to keep them upright.

20

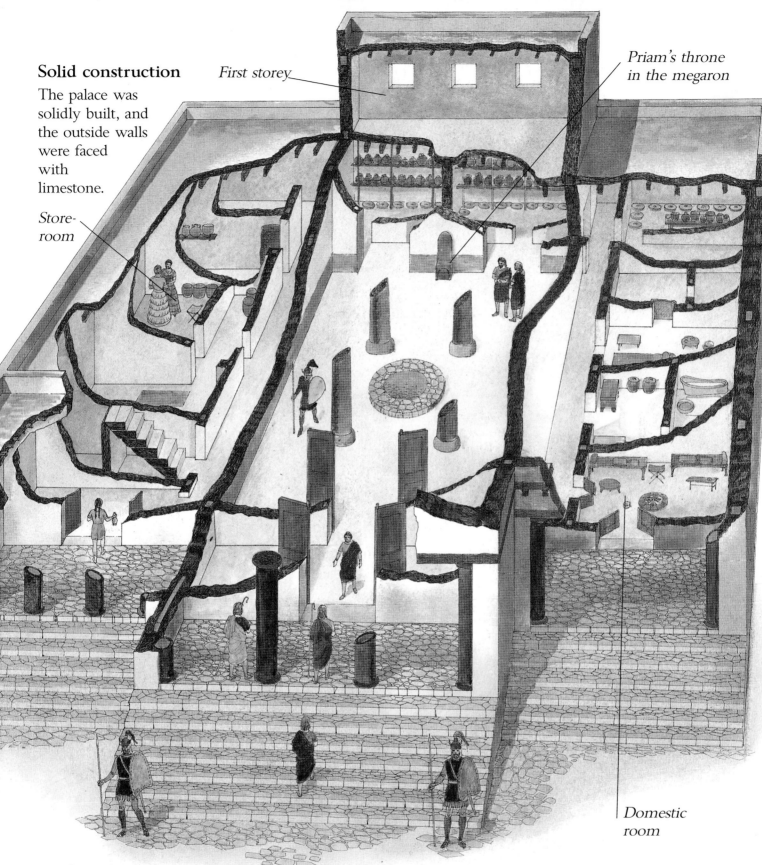

Solid construction

The palace was solidly built, and the outside walls were faced with limestone.

First storey

Store-room

Priam's throne in the megaron

Domestic room

Fit for a king

The palace was two storeys high, and would have measured about 30 by 15 metres (100 by 50 feet) Inside there was a hall on the ground floor called a "megaron", with a large fireplace at the centre. Around the hall were storerooms, domestic quarters and workshops.

Interior decoration

The interiors of the state rooms were finely plastered, carved and painted with geometric patterns and scenes from nature.

Ruling Troy

Most of the evidence for the existence of Priam's palace is based on guesswork - archaeologists have never been able to establish whether King Priam was a real man or just a figure in mythology. However the fine palaces found by Schliemann and his successors among the ruins at Troy show that whoever did rule the city was very powerful, wealthy and established.

Because the inner city area of Troy is fairly small, experts originally thought that the King of Troy probably only ruled over a few thousand people. But recently archaeologists discovered a lower city, beyond the walls and extending to the east and south, which was probably home to thousands more. The kingdom of Troy must have been strong, powerful and of great importance to the entire region.

If Troy was governed like other city-states of the time, its powerful ruler would have been helped by a group of chiefs. These positions were hereditary and those who held them were called the "aristoei" - the aristocracy. Beneath them in the social order came traders, craftsmen, labourers, women and finally, at the bottom of the pile, slaves.

Layered society

The structure of a Bronze Age society looked like a pyramid. The state was ruled by a "hierarchy". This was also reflected in the organization of the family, which was ruled by the father.

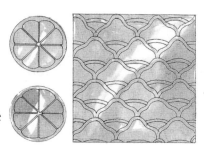

Trojan decoration
These decorative patterns were found at Troy. Similar patterns might have adorned the walls of the royal palace.

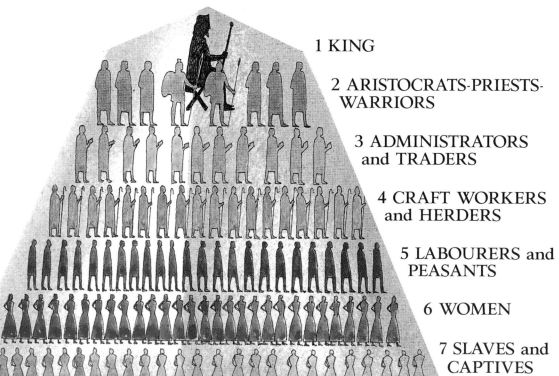

1 KING

2 ARISTOCRATS-PRIESTS-WARRIORS

3 ADMINISTRATORS and TRADERS

4 CRAFT WORKERS and HERDERS

5 LABOURERS and PEASANTS

6 WOMEN

7 SLAVES and CAPTIVES

History in music

The poet who sang with a lyre was called a "lyric poet". He sang about the deeds of kings and heroes to strengthen the community's sense of pride and to preserve the memory of important events. The lyric poet played an important role in promoting the King and spreading news. The story of the Trojan War was probably sung by lyric poets for hundreds of years before people wrote it down.

Heart of the palace

The King and his advisers held council meetings in the *megaron*, or great hall of the palace, where the king had his throne.

Ordinary lives

Priam's palace was built upon a walled terrace on the highest ground in the city. Around it, on the lower terrace, were the houses of the nobles.

During the later period of Priam's Troy, the simpler houses of craft workers, traders, labourers and servants were crowded together along narrow streets huddled against the inner walls of the city.

The craft workers worked for the royal family and the nobility. Women spun wool and wove cloth, ground grain and peas for flour and prepared food. Slaves and servants worked long hours catering to the nobility. The greater part of the population, including the farmers, herders and most of the labourers, lived outside the city in the open countryside.

A bustling city

As the population of Priam's Troy increased, craft workers and labourers built their simple houses quickly against the walls of the city. In between were narrow dark alleys.

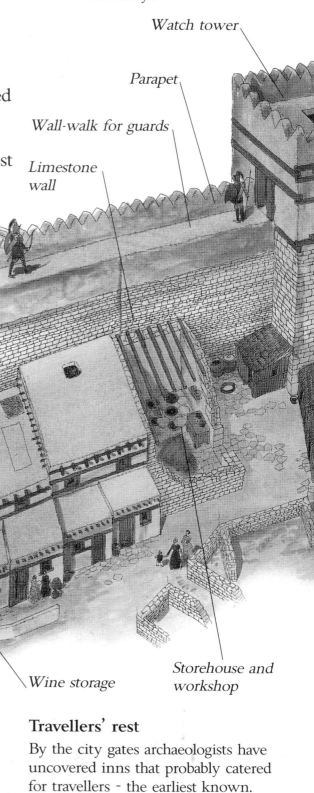

Watch tower

Parapet

Wall-walk for guards

Limestone wall

Gateway

Wine storage

Inn

Typical family dwelling

Storehouse and workshop

Travellers' rest

By the city gates archaeologists have uncovered inns that probably catered for travellers - the earliest known.

Greek loom

Loom weights

Spindle-whorls

Bone augers and sewing needles

Bronze pins and sewing needles

Wool weavers

Thousands of spinning and weaving implements found by archaeologists at Troy strongly hint of a thriving cottage industry in making wool cloth. Although no trace has been found of any loom, archaeologists assume the device would have been similar to prehistoric and Greek looms.

At home

An ordinary family - grandmother, mother and child, around a typical Trojan domestic fireplace.

Woman using a spindle to make wool thread

Dipper and three-legged cooking pot

Amphora for water

Five-wick oil lamp

Plates

Decanter in the shape of an animal

Ceramic legacy

Schliemann and his successors unearthed many pots and ceramic objects at Troy.

25

Farming

Beyond the city walls the houses of farmers and labourers stood in the open countryside, surrounded by fields, orchards and vineyards that belonged to the king. Here farmers grew food and reared animals for meat, work and warfare.

Today, Mediterranean farmers grow wheat and produce olive oil and wine. Trojan agriculture was much the same. Nothing of Troy's agricultural life remains, for unlike the work of craftsmen, agriculture leaves few traces that survive the centuries.

Rearing horses

Horse breeding was an important activity in Troy. The superior quality of Trojan horses is known from later historical accounts. Another clue to the importance of the horse is that many pottery handles found at Troy were modelled as horses' heads.

Horse breeders try to tame a wild horse

Woman picking olives

Goats and sheep

Sheep and goat farming was one of the main activities in the Trojan countryside. The sheeps' wool was spun and woven by the women of Troy.

Preparing the land

The soil was good for growing things, but the weather was harsh and archaeologists think it unlikely that any irrigation system supplied water to the crops.

Tilling (digging) the soil was probably done by hand, using wooden hoes hardened in the fire. Simple tools like this have been found in other Bronze Age cities.

Head covering gave protection from the blazing sun

A Trojan farmer tills the soil with a hardened piece of wood

Outside the great walls of Troy, "lower Troy" was protected by simple fortifications. War and invasion were always a threat and, despite the importance of farming, every able-bodied man had to go to war whenever the King commanded. A good time to attack an enemy was just as their crops were ripening. Destroying the crops meant they would face food shortages, and even starvation, in the coming winter.

Simple ploughs

Teams of oxen pulled simple ploughs, which scratched the ground to create a furrow (shallow trench) for planting.

Harvest time

Crops were harvested with sickles made of deer antler or horn with a cutting edge made of flints.

Crafts and trades

Schliemann's many discoveries reveal the great skill of Troy's craft workers. Although the gold and silver artefacts are the most spectacular items, some of the pottery is also outstanding.

Schliemann was the first to recognize that pottery tells us more about the past than gold. Only the wealthy owned gold objects, but pottery was used by everyone.

Intricate designs on pots allow archaeologists to recognize Trojan pottery even in the ruins of faraway cities. The extent of Trojan trade links became clear as pottery from King Priam's time was recovered throughout the Aegean. This indicates both extensive trading activities and great wealth for the city.

Fancy vessels

Schliemann discovered these gold vessels in Priam's treasure.

Bronze objects

Trojan craft workers cast these bronze tools and weapons using moulds:
1 arrowheads
2 scraper
3 table knives

Wandering smiths

Ancient smiths were a class of people apart. Like gypsies they travelled from town to town offering their skills.

Double mould

Simple stone mould

Furnace

Bellows

Cross-section through a smelting furnace

Casting a spear head

To make a spear head, a smith poured molten metal into a double mould. When cool, the smith separated the two halves and removed the casting.

Making a cup

Craft workers hammered a disc of gold onto a mandrel to form a cup.

Gold disc

Smelting

An alloy is a combination of two or more metals. To make bronze, copper and tin were melted in a charcoal furnace. Bellows blew air through the fire, making it burn hotter.

Mandrel

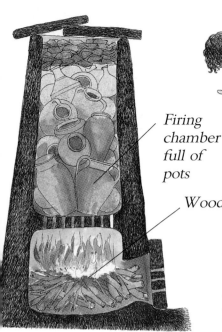

Firing chamber full of pots

Wood fire heats kiln

Making a jar

To make one of the large storage jars found in Priam's Troy, potters first made the two halves, then stuck them together before firing.

Firing pottery

To make clay vessels hard enough to withstand everyday use, they need to be fired in a kiln (potter's oven). Trojan kilns were tall and cone shaped.

Stone wheel

Pots on display

A selection of typical Trojan pottery. The flask on the right at the front is Mycenaean, and was probably imported from Greece.

Turning the wheel

An assistant turned the potter's wheel, helping to make smaller clay items.

A good find

Schliemann himself found this amazing vase. In his diary he wrote: "It is a glistening red and baked right through."

Amphora art

Before firing, pots could be decorated. Here an artist decorates an amphora with distinctive patterns.

In the workshop

Trojan potters made mid-sized vessels by stacking coils of clay, then smoothing them with water.

29

Religion

Archaeology deals with physical remains. The work of archaeologists shows you what sort of houses people lived in, what they ate and perhaps what they wore. But unless a people were able to write and their written records are discovered, you cannot know what they thought and believed.

Small marble idols found at Troy

Some written material has been found at Troy. This mainly takes the form of simple lists that catalogue goods stored in the King's warehouses and in workshops. However, a few clay tablets have been found which appear to have the names of Trojan gods inscribed on them. The tablets have been found at the foot of shrines where offerings would have been made to the deities.

The names of the gods are almost identical to those of deities from later Greek times, known to us through history, literature and mythology. The Trojan Bronze Age idols are rather simply made compared to later, more sophisticated Greek statues. But archaeologists believe they are meant to represent the same gods as were worshipped centuries later.

Bronze figurine of a deity from early Troy

Clues in clay

A written clay tablet from Pylos, Greece. Such tablets often carry the names of Greek gods including Zeus, Hera and Dionysos.

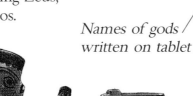

Names of gods written on tablet

Snake woman

This figurine of the "Snake goddess" was unearthed in Crete.

Sacred find

This gold ornament comes from Mycenae in Greece. It represents an altar.

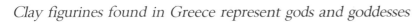

Clay figurines found in Greece represent gods and goddesses

Idols by the tower

Outside the tower of Ilios archaeologists found a number of pedestals. Experts believe that these supported crude statues of idols - the gods of Troy.

Scaean gate

Tower of Ilios

Pedestal supported idol

Trojan god

Wall of city

Burnt offerings

Next to Troy's main gate Schliemann discovered a building that was used as a shrine. Offerings to the gods - consisting of burning foods and delicacies - were made in front of the idols on the outside walls as well as within the shrine.

Some offerings were left at the base of the pillar

Troy at war

According to Homer's *Iliad* Helen, the beautiful wife of Menelaus, King of Sparta, was kidnapped by Paris, eldest son of Priam, King of Troy. To avenge this insult and bring Helen back, Agamemnon, Menelaus's brother, brought together the greatest leaders of Greece and attacked Troy.

The city finally fell after a ten-year siege and many deaths. The *Iliad* ends when Hector, the youngest son of Priam, is killed by Achilles.

Soldiers defend tower of Ilios and the Scaean gate

Battle rages

This scene depicts the battle for Troy as it really might have appeared. A leader, possibly Achilles, exhorts his men while archers, swordsmen and slingers attack the city's defenders.

Armour could be heavy and cumbersome

Whatever happened at Troy, the event that destroyed the city must have been of great importance to the people of the time - it led Homer to create what is one of the greatest works of literature in history.

Many centuries after the Trojan War, Greek colonists built a city on the ruins of Troy. Alexander the Great, Augustus and Caesar all visited the city that had risen upon the one that Homer described.

Cheek piece

Arms and armour

The warriors on both sides of the Trojan War wore armour and carried spears, swords and daggers. Bronze Age warfare did not include cavalry - the chariot was the war machine of the princely hero.

Tusk helmets

Trojan helmets are mentioned by Homer. They were made out of rows of boar's tusks.

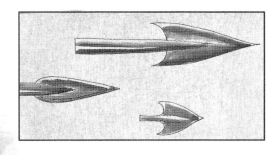

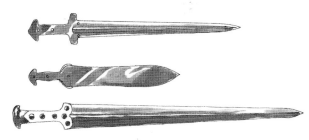

Deadly points

Arrowheads found at Troy were possibly fired during the long siege.

Edged weapons

Swords and daggers during the Trojan War were made from sharpened bronze.

Into battle

Warfare frequently found its way into art. This Mycenaean vase painting depicts a soldier escorting a charioteer and driver to the battlefield. Chariots normally had a two-person crew.

Off to war

The Achaean army leaves for Troy while a woman waves farewell. Foot soldiers were lightly dressed and carried a spear, shield, sword and dagger. From a painted vase found by Schliemann at Mycenae, in Greece.

The legacy of Troy

According to Virgil's *Aeneid*, the Trojan War ended when the Achaeans constructed a huge wooden horse and left it outside the city walls. Intrigued, the Trojans took it into the city. That night, Achaean soldiers hiding in the horse jumped out, opened the gates and let their army into Troy. Caught off guard, the Trojans were defeated and their city was destroyed.

Schliemann, like other scholars, originally believed the ancient writings described real events. But, as more and more ancient Greek sites were excavated the evidence indicated otherwise. Today scholars agree that the story of the Trojan Horse is a myth.

The Trojan Horse on a Greek vase of 750BC, about the time Homer was alive. The myth was as popular in the ancient world as it is today.

A stirring tale

The story of the wooden horse has fired imaginations for more than 2,000 years.

Troops left the horse through a trapdoor

The story of the Trojan Horse

(adapted from the *Aeneid* of Virgil)

The Achaeans, realizing that Troy could not be captured by force, decided to play a trick. They built a huge horse out of wood, and within it they sealed a team of hand-picked soldiers. Then the Achaean fleet sailed away to the island of Tenedos, where they hid. The Trojans, believing the Achaeans had given up and gone home, joyously opened the gates of Troy and flocked to see the deserted Achaean camp.

The great horse remained outside the walls while the Trojans argued over what to do with it. Some people thought that it should be dragged into the city and set up in the citadel. Others believed the horse should be destroyed. Hearing the commotion, Laocoön, a priest, ran from the palace with a great crowd, and cried out: "Citizens, what madness is this? Do you really believe the Achaeans have left? Do you think that any gift left by the enemy is free of treachery? Beware of Greeks bearing gifts!"

In spite of the priest's warning, everyone now said that the horse must be brought to its rightful place in the heart of the city. All set to work fixing wheels under its feet, and tying ropes around its neck. Boys and girls chanted hymns and helped pull on the ropes, wheeling the huge structure into the centre of Troy.

As these events unfolded, the Achaean squadron set sail from Tenedos and by that night was anchored off the coast of Troas. When the royal galley gave the signal - a tongue of flame - Sinon, a traitor planted in the city by the Achaeans, opened the trapdoor in the belly of the horse. This freed the soldiers inside. Sliding down ropes, the Achaeans spread throughout the sleeping city. They killed the watchmen and opened the gates of Troy to the troops arriving from the galleys. Troy was set on fire and razed to the ground.

Lost and found

What happened to Priam's treasure? Schliemann smuggled the hoard out of Turkey without letting the Turkish government know, and transported it to Germany, where it was put on display in Berlin.

When Berlin was invaded by the Allies at the end of World War II, the treasure vanished and nothing was heard about it for 50 years.

Then, in 1996, the whole treasure, intact and in all its glory, was put on show at the Pushkin Museum in Moscow. Once again, archaeologists around the world were amazed by the fine quality of the craftsmanship.

Rose decoration

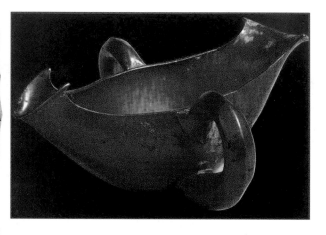

Gold boat-shaped cup

Gold spherical vase

Precious pin

This great gold pin is decorated with a rose and spiral motif.

Amazing vessels

Each of these graceful containers is wrought from sheets of gold (see p 28). They are a testament to the skill of the Trojan craft workers.

Valuable jewellery

These heavy gold earrings were each made from a thin, coiled gold cylinder.

Noble decoration

This gold armlet is decorated with spirals made from gold wire. It would have adorned a noblewoman of Troy.

Six-ringed earring

Three-ringed earring

Spiral decoration was common in the ancient world

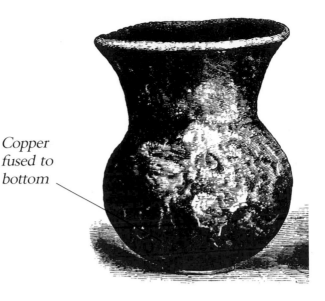

Copper fused to bottom

Solid silver vase

Schliemann and his workers found vases made from silver and gold/silver alloys during the excavation. The vessel shown here had a quantity of copper fused to its bottom by the heat of the fire that destroyed the city.

Stunning headdress

A diadem was a beautifully ornate headdress. Schliemann found two in Priam's treasure. The illustration above is from Schliemann's book *Troy and its remains*, and shows the larger of the diadems. It is made of 16,000 tiny pieces of gold chain, leaves and pendants.

Small but magnificent

Schliemann found a smaller diadem as well. The picture on the right shows a detail of it.

A fine object

Not all objects Schliemann unearthed were made of gold. The finely crafted ritual hammer-axe, below, is made from blue azurite stone.

Fancy fastening

This gold pin is decorated with spiral motifs and small vases.

Panels of spiral motifs

Chronology

Lyre

BC

circa 3600 Seafaring people arrive on the coast of Troas.

c 3000 First known fortified site built at Troy, now called Troy I by archaeologists.

c 2500 Troy I destroyed and a new settlement, Troy II, built. This is the city Schliemann believed was Homer's Troy and in which he found "Priam's treasure".

c 2200 Troy II destroyed and Troy III built on its ruins.

c 2050 Troy III destroyed and Troy IV built on the site.

c 1900 Troy IV destroyed and a new city, Troy V, built.

Gold ornament

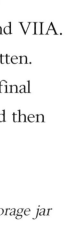

c 1800 Troy VI built on the site of Troy V. Wilhelm Dorpfeld believed that this was Homer's Troy, although it was destroyed, c 1300, by an earthquake and not by the Greeks as Homer recounted in his works.

c 1300 Troy VII ravaged by fire, rebuilt by the survivors, destroyed around 1200 BC, perhaps by the Greeks, and finally abandoned about 1000 BC. Most archaeologists now believe the second phase of this city, known as Troy VIIA, is the Troy of the Trojan wars.

c 700 Troy VIII built on the abandoned site of Troy VII and VIIA.

c 700 The *Iliad* probably written.

c 500 Troy IX built. In this final phase Troy is first a Greek and then a Roman city.

c 335 Alexander the Great visits Troy.

Making a storage jar

AD

c 1160 The French poet, Benoît de Sainte-Maure, writes his long poem, *Le Roman de Troie*. The story of Troy continued to fascinate people.

1711 Anne Davier translates the *Iliad* into French.

1822 Birth of Heinrich Schliemann in Ankershagen, eastern Germany.

1836 Schliemann leaves school and starts work in a grocer's shop.

Heinrich Schliemann

1850s Californian gold rush. Schliemann travels to the USA, starts a bank in Sacramento and makes a fortune.

1853-6 The Crimean War. Schliemann makes another fortune.

1868 Schliemann visits Troas for the first time. He is convinced that Hissarlik is the site of Troy.

1869 (March) Schliemann becomes an American citizen.

1869 (September) Schliemann marries Sophia Kastromenos.

1871 Schliemann is given permission by the Turkish government to start digging at Hissarlik.

1873 Schliemann discovers "Priam's treasure".

1880 Schliemann smuggles his Trojan treasures to Germany; they are kept in Berlin.

Clay figurines

1890 Death of Heinrich Schliemann.

1932 Death of Sophia Schliemann.

1945 At the end of World War II, German museums and art galleries are looted by the victorious Soviet army.

Trojan vase

1991 Russians acknowledge the looting for the first time.

1993 Russians admit that they have "Priam's treasure".

1996 Russians display the treasure to the public.

Glossary

Achaeans Ancestors of the ancient Greeks, the Achaeans fought the Trojans in the ten-year Trojan War.

Aeneid An epic poem by the Roman writer Virgil, describing the adventures of the Trojan hero Aeneas.

amphora A large pottery storage jar; used for water or wine.

Trojan woman picking olives

antiquarian A nineteenth-century word for an archaeologist.

aristoei The ancient Greek word for "aristocracy" and the term used to describe hereditary chiefs who helped rulers like King Priam to govern the city-states.

artefact An object made by humans; in an archaeological context artefacts are the objects made by ancient civilizations.

Athens The leading city-state in mainland ancient Greece and Troy's great rival.

auger A tool that bores holes.

bronze An alloy, or combination of metals, made from copper and tin. Used to make weapons and tools in the ancient world.

city-state A city that governs itself and the land immediately around it.

Dardanelles The narrow strait that links the Aegean Sea to the Sea of Marmara. According to Homer, the Dardanelles was the site of Charybdis, a huge and dangerous whirlpool, and the home of Scylla, a terrible six-headed monster.

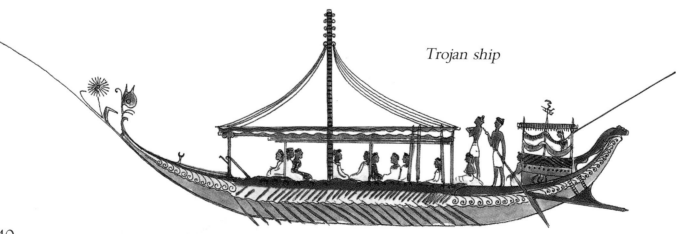

Trojan ship

Homer The blind poet who may or may not have written the *Iliad* and the *Odyssey*. The ancient Greeks thought he did; modern scholars are not so sure, although they believe that the *Iliad* was written around 700BC.

Iliad The great epic poem, perhaps written by Homer, that describes the wars between the Greeks and the Trojans.

lyre An ancient "U"-shaped stringed musical instrument.

lyric poet An ancient poet who sang his works while playing a lyre. Lyric poets sang about wars, myths and adventures.

mandrel A post-like tool, used by craftsmen to make flat sheets of metal into three-dimensional objects.

megaron The great hall in an ancient Greek or Trojan palace.

Mount Olympus The highest mountain in Greece and the home, according to the ancient Greeks, of their gods.

Odyssey The sequel to the *Iliad*, it recounts the fall of Troy and the long homeward journey of the Greek hero Odysseus.

parapet An upwards extension of the top of a wall, designed to protect soldiers standing on the wall-walk from attack.

sickle A "C"-shaped tool with a sharpened edge, used to harvest crops such as wheat.

Sparta Another Greek city-state; a rival of Athens.

Troas The plain in north-western Turkey overlooked by the city of Troy.

Ulysses The Roman form of the name Odysseus.

wall-walk The flattened top of a wall, located behind the parapet, built so that soldiers can walk along it.

Achaean warrior in armour

Heroes of Troy

Scholars believe the characters and events recorded in the *Iliad* and other ancient works are a mixture of truth and myth. However, Homer's heroes became the object of a religious cult in Greece; their deeds were celebrated in great literature, paintings and sculptures. Here are some of the principal characters in the story of the Trojan War.

Helen

All fought for her

Helen, the beautiful wife of King Menelaus of Sparta, was, according to legend, abducted by Paris, the son of King Priam of Troy, and carried off to that city. Many of the kings and heroes of Greece led by Agamemnon, the brother of Menelaus, took up arms and went to rescue Helen. There followed the bitterly fought ten years' war, ending with the fall of Troy. Helen was so attractive that she became known as "the face that launched a thousand ships" - referring to the number of vessels in the Achaean fleet.

Agamemnon
King of Mycenae; commanded the army that besieged Troy.

Ajax
A great Achaean warrior; claimed Achilles's armour after his death.

Achilles
Hero of the Iliad; killed Hector and was later himself killed by Paris.

Paris
Son of Priam; abducted Helen, an action which began the war.

Priam
Trojan king and father of 50 sons; killed on the night Troy fell.

Hector
Troy's defender; killed by Achilles at the end of Homer's Iliad.

Index

Index

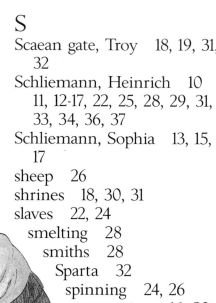

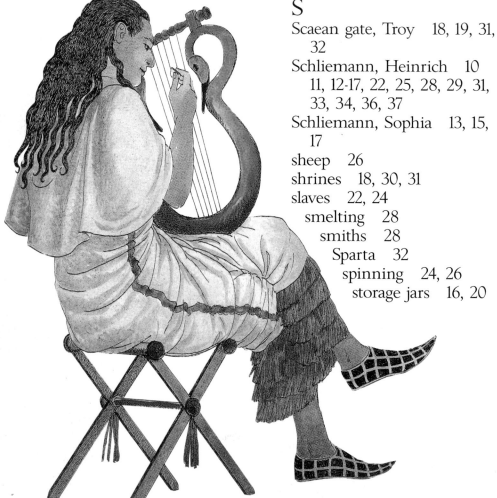